HER HAIR
PLAYS WITH FIRE

poems by

Mary M. Sesso

Finishing Line Press
Georgetown, Kentucky

HER HAIR
PLAYS WITH FIRE

For my family

ACKNOWLEDGMENTS

Grateful acknowledgement is made to the following publications in which
these poems appeared:

Cardinal Magazine: "Thanksgiving," "The First Day Of Winter"
Chrysanthemum Review; "Red Noise," "Apple Orchard"
Comstock Review: "Wanting," "Strawberries," "First Loves"
Helen Literary Magazine: "Patterns," "Why I Want You Beside Me When I'm
Dying"
Loch Raven Review: "Dinner Companion," "Looking For My Muse," "Let Me
Tell You," "Her Hair Plays With Fire"
Medical Literary Messenger: "Age-Related Macular Degeneration"
"The Evening Shift," "Thirteen"
Rat's Ass Review: "What We Didn't Know"

My workshop friends Kazimieras Kampe, Byron Nesland, Philip Wexler,
Luther Jett's First Saturday group, the Federal Poets, Moira Egans's
workshops, deserve many thanks for their help in crafting these poems.

Publisher: Leah Huete de Maines
Editor: Christen Kincaid
Cover Art: Jerilyn Sodee
Author Photo: Lisa M. Sodee
Cover Design: Elizabeth Maines McCleavy

Order online: www.finishinglinepress.com
also available on amazon.com

Author inquiries and mail orders:
Finishing Line Press
PO Box 1626
Georgetown, Kentucky 40324
USA

Table of Contents

We don't see things as they are. We see them as we are.
Anais Nin

Looking For My Muse

He used to cling to my neck. We would spend all day in bed,
a day of delirium, sweat and crumpled sheets.
When night unfurled, there were no regrets.

I look for him in the dark sky but it's hard to see with high-
flying clouds chasing the dirty moon's face. I look into night's
edge. Is that him slinking away, hiding under a street lamp?

If only I could stew in both pleasure and pain
sipping wine on the front porch, maybe in this year of loss
he would burst forth and blossom like a thorny rose.

I set out books and journals as decoys, play Monk,
Duke and Ella, even promise to marry the next weedy flower
that stirs in the sun if only he'd show up.

Forgetting and age are a formidable pair. If muse is to return,
he must wipe my foggy glasses, dig up ruby, jade, and lapis
secrets Then I'll make a mosaic out of all gems he leaves me.

Bada Boom Begonias
for Eric

I hear their color call
from down the street.
These flowers
with their yellow throats
and heart-shaped leaves
shout *Look at me!*
My children yelled
the same thing
when they learned
to pump up the swing
higher and higher.
Look at me, Ma!
I was afraid
daredevil Eric
would go over the top
and fly out.
Years later on my birthday
he sent me flowers
in boisterous shades of rose,
so pleased with himself
he wrote on the card
Look at these, Ma!
Their fragrance
still colors the air.
I inhale.

July

This dyspeptic grudge of heat,
hot enough to kill,
fools me into hoping that tomorrow
robins will pack up their notes,
move out and leave us all safe
in cool fall air.
Something unsafe
hides and thrives
in this marathon
of sweat.
It sneaks out of one body
into another, flames up
with fever and cough
and stinks of death.
It's as though at any second
a carelessly thrown lawn dart
could pierce my heart.
I brew resentment
behind closed doors, wish
for cold days when the earth
will tilt and expose me
to the clean face of the moon.

Dinner Companion

Halfway through the soup course
my ears wish they were
somewhere else.
His words, gray as his beard,
ramble, grow mold,
take over the entire table,
leaving mine stuck
in my throat.
A bawling baby
and a dropped tray
of silverware make
the air flinch, swallowing
me whole.
By dessert his monologue
has scaled the mountain
of monotony. As we stand
to leave, he grows tired.
Silence tumbles down
loud as a shattered glass
and suddenly I remember
how loneliness can leave you
feeling naked with only words
to cover yourself.

Musing At The Eatery

Does the man at the next table
wear a "Blessed" sign across both sleeves
because when he goes to confession
his sins have zero gravity and penance
is never more than three Hail Marys,
because cheating never enters through
his heart or hands or chest when he
plays cards with his buddies,
because he does his best not to let
his mind somersault and silently sing
Slow Boat To China during the sermon,
because he might give lust a bad name
when he stares at his neighbor's breasts,
aware his eyes should have no entry,
or maybe it's because his guardian angel
is all thigh and calf and wears a wedding band
with his name inscribed inside.

Strawberries

The strawberry red dress
with spaghetti straps
the young woman wears
at the café shows her
breasts struggling to be free.
It would have been called sexy
underwear from Frederick's
of Hollywood back in the fifties
when *risqué* was kept behind
closed doors.

The strawberry in my salad
doesn't owe me a thing.
But its redness, when cut in half,
looks like a cut-opened heart.
If my heart were to open,
a deep blushing secret
would fall out, how a strapless
gown with a strapless bra failed
while I was dancing to Jimmy Dorsey's
Boogie Woogie at a college gala,
leaving my breasts astonished.

Apple Orchard

It begins like this: sometime
after dark, deer show up silent
as flurrying snow to eat the sour,
wormy apples half buried
in icy mud.

I watch from the window—
The moon licks away
the deer's color,
leaving them bone-pale,
almost silvery.
I feel like I'm the center of the universe.
Creatures the color of the moon
move in and out under trees
just for my pleasure.

Too soon clouds let loose darkness
and I retreat into winter
where the sound of hooves
striking the ground is forbidden,
where quiet is endless and perfect.

Orange and Black

Winter is not a season, it's an occupation.
—*Sinclair Lewis*

Enough of snowflakes and cold.
The snow's hands are heavy,
grimy gray and old and hold
down my forsythia as if it's kneeling

on a hard pew, covering up
two yellow blossoms. If I could
carry a tune, I'd sing gray a requiem,
while wishing for spring and dogwood

blooms, or waiting for the Baltimore oriole
to sing, a lyric tenor gussied up
in black and orange, colors so wild
you'd think sunset and night stole

each other's drama. Enough of wind and ice,
time to beckon the sun, not wish away my life.

Stillness

Is caught in the eyes of the deer
my father shot, hanging by its neck
in the garage, in a grasshopper
on the sidewalk half-eaten by ants,
and there, in the corner, a piece
of brownie I forgot to sweep up.

I can tell you when I don't see it:
in the evening when I walk the dog
and the moon won't stay put, when
milkweed thickens the wind with fluff,
and when the muscle of your breathing
makes the sheet flutter. Of course
I can make stillness, too. I hold out
my hand, catch some sun dazzle
and let it warm my fingers like a glove.

Let Me Tell You

About the jay tearing apart a mouse
and eating it. I had to stop watching.
Did you know the jay's feathers
tell a lie? They're just gray. Light refraction
makes them look blue.

Have I ever mentioned the time
my mother flew up into a baby buggy
when she saw a mouse and screamed
for me to get a broom and kill it? I chased
the thing, beat it to death then threw up.

Another thing—There's a family of mice
living behind my blue Eve's Tears.
Do these lilies of the valley imagine
they're in a garden of Eden where
they're the heroes and smite a snake,

gods are absent and apples rare?
It's my garden, too, where you and I,
Adam and Eve, curl up to a future
redolent with *muguet*. Best of all,
I won't have to kiss you goodbye.

What We Didn't Know

The afternoon knows what the morning never suspected.
—Robert Frost

On the day we knew
how depressed she was,
she sat on the floor crying,
holding her Yorkie.
Her musk perfume gripped
the air so tight
it smothered the room.
Her outburst of smiles
would put a brake on tears
every so often,
a sign we took she would survive
and not need watching eyes.

What we didn't see
was the suitcase full of empty
vodka bottles hiding under a bed
or holes in the ceiling
from two practice shots
made by the rusty revolver
stashed under a pillow,
biding its time until
we kissed her goodbye
and went out the door.

Thirteen

It happened in my
grandfather's bedroom
in 1913 where his beloved
thirteen canaries sang,
which is to say they were trying
to drown out the siren
in his belly, pain that rubbed
his eyes raw with salt tears,
which is to say his ears
were trying to stop listening,
though there wasn't
enough cotton in the world
to stuff and muffle the sound,
which is to say the pain
was shouting louder, but
comfort from his medicine
cabinet over in the corner
was shouting even louder,
but before he swallowed
the last spoonful of opium,
and being a pharmacist
knowing there was no walking
back, he opened up the cages,
held each bird in his hand
and strangled every little bit
of yellow fluff.

Wanting

for Mara and Rome

I want to save something lovely for my last days,
the way my great granddaughter wants to pirouette
in her socks, the way azaleas want to bend to the sun.
I want something delightful as the rainbow living in the
driveway oil slick, something with gusto like the ladybug
buzzing on the window sill. If I could bank the song
of the mourning dove and my great grandson's whoop-
holler when he finds a spider, I would. I want to keep
the laughter at myself when my tongue twists on words
like mellifluous and cavernous, and when I mess up
directions for a cake mix. I want to remember love
as devoted as Superman's for Lois, as achingly tender
as Napoleon and Josephine's. The trick is to keep on saving
while stars save their shine for night, the sky saves pink
and purple for day, even as darkening unfolds.

Why I Want You Beside Me When I'm Dying

after Mary Makofske

Because you'll soft shoe your way in
wearing a cowboy hat crooning
I'll See You Again, saying it's easy
to stop breathing because you've done it.
Because your heart is immortal, and even if
my eyes are empty, you'll hold my hand.
Because you've written songs about sad folk
who're unlucky in love, but none were about me.
Because you'll whip out a rosary from your
back pocket and won't shame me but laugh
for forgetting how to say it. After I'm gone,
I want to be remembered if you see a spider web
laced with sunlit dew. And when you smile,
the sky will be blue.

The Evening Shift

I wonder what my patient sees?
She looks up but her eyes
don't track my finger.
I wonder how the cancer learned
to manufacture so much pain
now well muted by morphine?

Was it by paying close attention,
as if it could see to light up nerves
like they were cigarettes,
then letting them do a slow burn?
What about the sound her organs make—
Are they silent as a smoking gun
as the cancer eats their cells alive
until they're not there?
And I wonder what her eyes saw last?
Was it the pink and white sweet peas
outside the hospital? Millions of pink
and white flowers.

I tell her every day the orchid
her son sent is sweet and pretty
as a purple gem stone on a stem
and that he'll be here soon.
Can language move her imagination
without the need to listen?

A Tisket A Basket

*The 5-year cancer survival rate was 49%
in 1970. It increased to 67% by 2013.*

My mortuary basket,
a name tag for your wrist
and one for your toe,
you won't get lost
wherever you go.
Some peroxide, alcohol
and cloths of paper,
to clean up blood
or any whatever.

God forgive me the sing-songy words
I sing to myself to help ease stress.
Cancer quickened its pace this shift
and caught three of my patients.
Families' tears flood the ward.
Comfort needs spill out of my hands.
And the morgue won't apologize
for its gray insistence.

In this place, the dying know they live
with the dead.

Red Noise

It's the sound of the sun turning
dark and a blood moon spilling
over the earth, a red light in a window
filling the room with promises of delight,
the taste of regret on a cheater's
tongue after a hot, one-night stand,
the stain of sin on Mephistopheles'
gaudy red shirt and tights as he leads
Faust off stage into hell, the color of guilt
on Cain's bloody hands after killing Abel,
and the haze hovering above a rose in a stem vase
on the white table, which together play
like a symphony.

First Loves

I miss you but I don't want you back.
You sweet-talked into my silence quietly as a cloud
floating in the sky. But often your pride grew loud,
like thunder songs that bellowed in the wind.

Falling for someone new in the Sixties was easy,
like listening to Gilberto and Getz's bossa nova.
Each blue sensuous sax and guitar note
sent my arms and legs dancing without shame.

In the Eighties, Rachmaninoff's Piano Concerti
soared out of the radio, rising in crescendos
and scored the space where mind and body meet
as if I were one of the keys being played.

My love today is a room without sun and sound.
No matter, because it can't match a moon
full of silver. *Luna, mira me.* Lie down with me
and not the tiger lilies, as I hum myself to sleep.

Thanksgiving

For chocolate to be Belgian and whole roasted.
For a bottomless glass of milk standing by.
For the recipe to be your grandmother's.

For vanilla flavor to be subtle.
For flour in a bag that warns of weevils.
For the gift of blades to cream butter and sugar.

For eggs to give up their yolks without resistance.
For flowers a cookie cutter finds in dough.
For the oven to scent the house with everything nice.

For a hot mitt to slide into the sink.
For your mother to warn tongues burn if you taste too soon.
For your aunt who gave you her heirloom serving platter.

For a hill of crumbs on your pink plate.
For sticky lips and fingers to wait for a damp cloth.
For the afternoon to have faded while you were eating.

For a low hanging winter sun to play in your hair,
For the image to turn up in your dream
and shine through your sleep.

Patterns

Water takes the shape
of whatever holds it,
the way milk takes the shape
of a mother's breast,
the way cancer arranges itself
in the shape of that breast,
stealing its loveliness,
hurt stealing its touch,
the way a woman's world
takes the shape of a coffin,
the way saying goodbye
takes the shape
of a High Requiem,
as tears take the shape
of black rosary beads,
hanging on decade
after decade
waiting for sickle-moons
to turn full and blue,
eyes finally drying
in its comforting light.

Student Nurse: Ypsilanti State Hospital
For The Mentally Ill, 1953

In 1980 Infantile autism is listed in the
Diagnostic and Statistical Manual for
the first time.

He spends the day sitting on the floor
rocking back and forth and hums—
he stares at nothing, just hums, and winces

if touched. It's like he lives in a parallel universe
plastered with Keep Out signs. Speech
is left outside the door and if a loud noise

barges in, he plugs his ears with index fingers
and moans. But Ben will smile if someone puts
a cigarette between his lips which he smokes

down to ash then stubs out on his arm,
watches it sear the flesh, not flinching,
as though he were covered with stone.

Last week the attendant with bad teeth
yelled *Ben, stop that fuckin' humming.*
Startled, Ben dropped his lunch tray.

You might guess how this ends, how the attendant
shot his fist into Ben's jaw just as I passed by,
how I shouted *Stop It*, how the attendant told me

to shut up or he'd slug me, too. Can you also guess
that Ben never uttered a sound, just stood there,
his jaw filling his hand?

When I filed an abuse report, the Director of Nurses
called me to her office where she threw questions at me
over and over:

Are you sure you want to sign this? You're positive?
Do you know what you're doing to a man's career?
Yes. Yes. Yes. I say.

No. The attendant wasn't fired.
Though for the rest of my rotation I left the sticky
fingerprints of a snitch wherever I went.

What Snow Brings

The death of a loved one is like amputation.
—C.S. Lewis

Friday:
A winter storm watch:
I shudder and your dying chills me.
All afternoon I rub your cheeks
and forehead. *"Your hand feels so cold,"*
you murmur over and over.

Sunday:
Snow is coming. I smell it, taste it.
Honey, drink this milk, I say,
but your eyes roll upwards. Suddenly I feel
as if you had weaned yourself and flown away
to a new life. I'm greedy, want love to fly you back.
La donna 'e mobile—
"You adore it, remember?" I turn up the volume.

Tuesday:
I see your face grow smaller and paler.
You're becoming lost like the afternoon sun.
Dear lord, I'm tired of waiting for snow.
I want to pull it over me and whitewash
everything that's ugly.

Wednesday:
The first flakes begin to fall.
I call your name again and again
while I stroke your arm,
but you're lost in a field of white.

The sky repeats the ground.
Unable to grasp the night,
I look for a path to follow,
but there is none.

The First Day Of Winter

Like a funeral director
the first day of winter
shows up in a black coat—
All of autumn's mock leaf color
has been embalmed in brown.
Summer's fat sun with its white
light and slow dance has been
put on ice and sent south.
In the meantime, spring
stands behind a velvet rope
like a mourner, memories
of a lilac mouth and forsythia arms
have faded and buried themselves.
Only when crocuses twitch below
the earth will winter let down its hair
and let them carve a path out of the snow.

Nurse Taking Care Of Her Father

How small he looks in the oxygen tent.
He has to pee. Right Now! How strange I feel
as I pull down the sheet to that dark place
and see the rumpled hospital gown
against scant white hair and wrinkled skin.

The warmth of his thighs enhances
my reluctance to know the nakedness
where I began. I slide the urinal between
his legs and pull the sheet back up.
You're all set, Papa.

He sighs, not concerned about modesty,
and confident my hand that's held
so many others teetering on life's edge,
won't let go of his when he enters
that space where I cannot go.

The Cooney Sisters

The stink of pee owned the air
stinging my nose when Mother and I
brought the Cooney sisters
a Christmas basket of food.
Those tiny wisps of white
must have been married to the odor
because they seemed content
with the yellow stained sheets drying
on the heater that blew only cold air.
I clung to my mother, but her perfume
couldn't kiss away the smell.
Our goodbyes were swift.
Even though I was shivering
I couldn't get outside soon enough
for the promise of fresh air.

Her Hair Plays With Fire

A girl watches her mother
who sits on the edge of the bed,
mirror in hand, brushing out
the coiled bun, counting out loud
one hundred strokes, sparks flying,
the mirror catching a setting sun
that glows in the west window.
The girl loves being in this moment.

During the day the mother wears
the silence of the dad's flannel shirts
and old lady coiled-up hair.
The girl suspects that if her mother
leaned toward the sun she'd bloom,
but it takes time for a girl to learn
rosy colors can alert suspicious eyes
and steal the peace.

Two Years Later

Within four months she lost a boy
who laughed and a baby who smiled.
Grief looks out of my mother's green eyes.
It's alive, always there and hungry,
licking up tears, an insatiable appetite
for salt. At night it slips under her eyelids
and steals her sleep.

On wet afternoons, when the world
is at its dreariest, her best friend
comes for coffee.
Sometimes they just sit in green silence
and wonder if grief is dying, wonder
when the moon will own the night,
and the sun will shed hard darkness.

The Color of Young Limes

So as not to disturb us
the willows drag themselves
out of winter quietly.
They begin in early March
when we're still asleep,
dipping their long arms
into a pool of green
rising up from their roots.
Ever so gently
they lean and swish,
surrounding themselves
with the color of young limes.
As the nights grow shorter,
a frenzy of darkling color
reaches fever pitch,
each tree believing it will be
the first to dazzle us awake.

Fear of Rejection

Big and gaudy,
the moon tonight
is my world.
I want to drive
right up to
that orange sphere,
sitting like a pumpkin
on the edge
of the horizon
and look in the window.
I want to see the dark
side, get to know it
before my life grows
any older and slides
into shadows, keeping
me from knowing
which world to enter.
Yet I sit in the car not
moving, knowing
the moon is busy
charming lovers
in the car next to mine,
and I would hate
to be told to stop
gawking and to please
butt out.

Though I'm Tired of Love Poems

I love you like a skinny iced latte
when I sweat scrubbing burnt pans,
like the way satin pants slide across my hips
when scales say I've lost three pounds.

I love you more because the cicada's
buzz silences the moon,
because you rescue me from the dark
before and after I disturb your dream,

because when gods are cankered,
and give us a hard kiss, we anchor
each other. Though I'm bored
when I sleep on my side of the bed,

and my heart sometimes labors,
it cheers up when it hangs onto metaphors.

Dear Disappointments

You know my name, you have
my number, but I've become weary
of our relationship.

Now, it's time to go.

Like I would for a dubious friend,
I will attend your funeral.
I want to make sure you're buried
and forever lie in peaceful *mortem*.
You can be next to memories
of old lovers, who are buried
in sweet forgetfulness. I won't mind.

You've been like an itch that can't be
scratched, a boil that won't burst.

You're like my old college sweatshirt
I've kept folded in my closet, torn
and faded, but can't bear to toss.

Again, it's time to go. Get up off your
knees. There will be no candles
or burning incense.

It's not been fun.

And please. Don't bother me
at night with your dreary cadence
of sleep-walkers.

Age-Related Macular Degeneration

To say there is choice is false.
 Blue. Green. Brown. Hazel. Gray. Liz Taylor's
  Violet. Colors tumble through the gene pool.
  .

Other eye genetics flex muscle
 and your age begins to crab what is perfect.
  Little by little your vision kneels before blindness

and stares into its abyss. Forever dims slowly.
 Your marvelous mind, packed with faces, flowers,
  words, has to live in a tight little world

made smaller and smaller as new sights refuse to appear,
 as if they have agreed to walk away.
  Blindness declares victory.

If you're dumb lucky, the last best image standing will be those daisies
 under your backyard fence, choked with yellow,
  their dark eyes looking back at you.

Mary Carolyn Sesso was born Mary Muehlmann and grew up in Michigan. She attended the Mercy School of Nursing, worked as a registered nurse until retirement and now sits on the Human Rights Committee at the National Children's Center. She holds a BA from the University of Maryland and an MFA from Vermont College. She is a member of the Writer's Center in Bethesda, Maryland, and is active in three poetry workshops. Her most recent work appeared in the *Coal Hill Review, Comstock Review, Helen Literary Magazine, Passager, The Medical Literary Messenger* and the *Gyroscope Review.*

"Dinner Companion" was nominated for a 2016 Pushcart Prize by the *Loch Raven Review.* Her first chapbook, *The Open Window,* was a finalist for the *Coal Hill Review* chapbook contest.

www.ingramcontent.com/pod-product-compliance
Lightning Source LLC
LaVergne TN
LVHW041327080426
835513LV00008B/620